20 best
grilling recipes

Houghton Mifflin Harcourt
Boston • New York • 2013

Copyright © 2013 by General Mills, Minneapolis, Minnesota. All rights reserved.

For information about permission to reproduce selections from this book, write to Permissions, Houghton Mifflin Harcourt Publishing Company, 215 Park Avenue South, New York, New York 10003.

www.hmhco.com

Cover photo: Lemon-Pepper Steaks (page 19)

General Mills
Food Content and Relationship Marketing Director: Geoff Johnson
Food Content Marketing Manager: Susan Klobuchar
Senior Editor: Grace Wells
Kitchen Manager: Ann Stuart
Recipe Development and Testing: Betty Crocker Kitchens
Photography: General Mills Photography Studios and Image Library

Houghton Mifflin Harcourt
Publisher: Natalie Chapman
Editorial Director: Cindy Kitchel
Executive Editor: Anne Ficklen
Associate Editor: Heather Dabah
Managing Editor: Rebecca Springer
Production Editor: Kristi Hart
Cover Design: Chrissy Kurpeski
Book Design: Tai Blanche

ISBN 978-0-544-31482-5
Printed in the United States of America

The Betty Crocker Kitchens seal guarantees success in your kitchen. Every recipe has been tested in America's Most Trusted Kitchens™ to meet our high standards of reliability, easy preparation and great taste.

FIND MORE GREAT IDEAS AT
BettyCrocker.com

Dear Friends,

This new collection of colorful mini books has been put together with you in mind because we know that you love great recipes and enjoy cooking and baking but have a busy lifestyle. So every little book in the series contains just 20 recipes for you to treasure and enjoy. Plus, each book is a single subject designed in a bite-size format just for you—it's easy to use and is filled with favorite recipes from the Betty Crocker Kitchens!

All of the books are conveniently divided into short chapters so you can quickly find what you're looking for, and the beautiful photos throughout are sure to entice you into making the delicious recipes. In the series, you'll discover a fabulous array of recipes to spark your interest—from cookies, cupcakes and birthday cakes to party ideas for a variety of occasions. There's grilled foods, potluck favorites and even gluten-free recipes too.

You'll love the variety in these mini books—so pick one or choose them all for your cooking pleasure.

Enjoy and happy cooking!

Sincerely,

Betty Crocker

contents

Burgers, Brats and More
Bacon-Cheeseburgers (Crowd Size) · 6
Foot-Long Coney Dogs · 7
Brats with Mustard Relish · 8
Italian Sausages with Peperonata · 9
Spicy Chili Bean Burgers · 10

Fiery Chicken
Taco-Spiced Chicken · 11
Three-Herb Chicken · 12
Firecracker Chicken Drummies · 13
Jerk Chicken Kabobs · 14

Surf and Turf
Spicy Coconut-Curry Shrimp · 15
Fish Tacos · 16
Seafood Packets with Lemon-Chive Butter · 17
Surf and Turf Kabobs · 18
Lemon-Pepper Steaks · 19
Pork Ribs with Smoky Barbecue Sauce · 20

Sizzling Sides
Easy Vegetables · 21
Greek Summer Squash · 22
Parmesan, Asparagus and Mushrooms · 23
Corn with Herb Butter · 24
Herbed New Potatoes · 25

Metric Conversion Guide · 26
Recipe Testing and Calculating Nutrition Information · 27

Burgers, Brats and More

Bacon-Cheeseburgers (Crowd Size)

Prep Time: 35 Minutes • **Start to Finish:** 35 Minutes • Makes 12 sandwiches

3 lb lean (at least 80%) ground beef
1 medium onion, finely chopped (½ cup)
¾ teaspoon pepper
12 hamburger buns, split
1 cup blue cheese dressing
12 slices bacon, crisply cooked, broken in half

1. Heat gas or charcoal grill. In large bowl, mix beef, onion and pepper. Shape into 12 patties, ¾ inch thick.

2. Place patties on grill over medium heat. Cover grill; cook 13 to 15 minutes, turning once, until meat thermometer inserted in center of patties reads 160°F. During last 2 minutes of cooking, place buns, cut side down, on grill until toasted.

3. Place burgers on bottom halves of buns. Top each burger with 4 teaspoons dressing and 2 pieces of bacon. Cover with top halves of buns.

1 Sandwich: Calories 460; Total Fat 28g (Saturated Fat 8g, Trans Fat 1.5g); Cholesterol 85mg; Sodium 610mg; Total Carbohydrate 24g (Dietary Fiber 1g); Protein 27g **Exchanges:** 1½ Starch, 3½ Medium-Fat Meat, 2 Fat **Carbohydrate Choices:** 1½

Tip No time for cooking bacon? Simply sprinkle cooked real bacon bits or pieces on the burgers instead!

Foot-Long Coney Dogs

Prep Time: 30 Minutes • **Start to Finish:** 30 Minutes • Makes 6 sandwiches

6 long hot dogs (each about 12 inches)
1 tablespoon butter or margarine, melted
1 can (15 oz) chili with beans
6 long hot dog buns, split
¾ cup shredded Cheddar cheese (3 oz)
1 large onion, chopped (1 cup), if desired

1 Heat gas or charcoal grill. In each hot dog, make crosswise diagonal cuts ½ inch apart and ¼ inch deep.

2 Carefully brush grill rack with vegetable oil. Place hot dogs on grill rack over medium heat. Grill uncovered 15 to 20 minutes, turning frequently and brushing occasionally with butter, until hot dogs are hot and slashes begin to open.

3 Remove label and top from can of chili. Add opened can of chili to grill for last 10 minutes of grilling, stirring occasionally, until hot. Serve hot dogs on buns with chili, cheese and onion.

1 Sandwich: Calories 660; Total Fat 37g (Saturated Fat 15g, Trans Fat 1.5g); Cholesterol 70mg; Sodium 2060mg; Total Carbohydrate 58g (Dietary Fiber 5g); Protein 24g **Exchanges:** 3 Starch, 1 Other Carbohydrate, 2 High-Fat Meat, 3½ Fat **Carbohydrate Choices:** 4

Tip Bermuda onions are exceedingly sweet and juicy, perfect for eating raw on "dogs" and burgers. They're available only in the summer months and are truly a treat to eat!

Brats with Mustard Relish

Prep Time: 30 Minutes • **Start to Finish:** 30 Minutes • Makes 4 sandwiches

1½ cups apple cider, beer or water

4 uncooked bratwurst (about 1 lb), thawed if frozen

½ teaspoon vegetable oil

1 slice (½ inch thick) sweet onion

⅓ cup chunky applesauce

2 tablespoons spicy brown mustard

4 brat or hot dog buns, split

1 Heat gas or charcoal grill. In 2-quart saucepan, heat cider to boiling. Add bratwurst; reduce heat to low. Cover; simmer 15 minutes.

2 Meanwhile, brush oil on cut side of onion. Place onion, oil side up, on grill over medium heat. Cover grill; cook 9 to 12 minutes, turning once, until onion is soft and edges are golden brown. Remove onion from grill; coarsely chop. In small bowl, mix onion, applesauce and mustard; set aside.

3 Drain bratwurst. Place on grill over medium heat. Cover grill; cook 6 minutes, turning once, until brown.

4 In each bun, place 1 bratwurst and about 2 tablespoons relish.

1 Sandwich: Calories 550; Total Fat 34g (Saturated Fat 12g, Trans Fat 1g); Cholesterol 70mg; Sodium 1450mg; Total Carbohydrate 44g (Dietary Fiber 2g); Protein 17g **Exchanges:** 2 Starch, 1 Other Carbohydrate, 1½ High-Fat Meat, 4 Fat **Carbohydrate Choices:** 3

Tip To save time, use fully cooked bratwurst and skip the simmering step. The sandwiches are delicious served with coleslaw, potato chips and fresh fruit.

Italian Sausages with Peperonata

Prep Time: 45 Minutes • **Start to Finish:** 45 Minutes • Makes 4 sandwiches

Sausages

- 4 uncooked hot or mild Italian sausage links (about 1 lb)
- 4 hot dog buns, split

Peperonata

- 2 medium yellow bell peppers, cut into ½-inch strips
- 2 medium red bell peppers, cut into ½-inch strips
- 1 large onion, sliced, separated into rings
- 2 cloves garlic, finely chopped
- 1 tablespoon chopped fresh or 1 teaspoon dried basil leaves
- 2 teaspoons chopped fresh or ½ teaspoon dried oregano leaves
- 1 tablespoon olive or vegetable oil
- 2 teaspoons lemon juice
- ½ teaspoon salt
- ¼ teaspoon pepper
- 1 can (3.8 oz) sliced ripe olives, drained

1 Heat gas or charcoal grill. Place sausages on grill over medium heat. Cover grill; cook about 25 minutes, turning occasionally, until no longer pink in center.

2 Meanwhile, in large bowl, toss all peperonata ingredients except olives; place in grill basket (grill "wok"). Place basket on grill with sausages; cook 5 to 8 minutes, shaking basket occasionally to turn vegetables, until bell peppers and onion are crisp-tender. Stir olives into peperonata.

3 Serve sausages on buns with peperonata.

1 Sandwich: Calories 520; Total Fat 31g (Saturated Fat 9g, Trans Fat 0g); Cholesterol 45mg; Sodium 1740mg; Total Carbohydrate 38g (Dietary Fiber 4g); Protein 22g **Exchanges:** 2 Starch, 1 Vegetable, 2 High-Fat Meat, 3 Fat **Carbohydrate Choices:** 2½

Tip If you have leftover peperonata, serve it on grilled steak sandwiches or fajitas.

Spicy Chili Bean Burgers

Prep Time: 25 Minutes • **Start to Finish:** 25 Minutes • Makes 5 sandwiches

1 cup Fiber One® original bran cereal

1 can (15 or 16 oz) spicy chili beans in sauce, undrained

½ cup quick-cooking oats

¼ cup chopped green onions (4 medium)

1 egg, slightly beaten

5 whole wheat burger buns, split

1¼ cups fresh baby spinach leaves

5 slices tomato

1 Place cereal in resealable food-storage plastic bag; seal bag and finely crush with rolling pin or meat mallet.

2 In medium bowl, mash beans with fork until no whole beans remain. Add cereal, oats, onions and egg; mix well. Shape mixture into 5 patties, 3½ inches in diameter.

3 Spray 12-inch skillet with cooking spray. Heat over medium heat. Add patties; cook about 10 minutes, turning once, until brown.

4 Place ¼ cup spinach and 1 tomato slice on bottom half of each bun; top with bean burger. Cover with top half of bun.

1 Sandwich: Calories 280; Total Fat 4.5g (Saturated Fat 1g, Trans Fat 0g); Cholesterol 40mg; Sodium 800mg; Total Carbohydrate 48g (Dietary Fiber 12g); Protein 11g **Exchanges:** 2½ Starch, ½ Other Carbohydrate, ½ Vegetable, ½ Fat **Carbohydrate Choices:** 3

Tip Legumes are loaded with plenty of fiber—the soluble kind. Start slowly so you have time to get used to added fiber in the diet!

Fiery Chicken

Taco-Spiced Chicken

Prep Time: 25 Minutes • **Start to Finish:** 25 Minutes • Makes 4 servings

- 2 tablespoons taco seasoning mix (from 1-oz package)
- 1 teaspoon dried oregano leaves
- 4 boneless skinless chicken breasts (about 1¼ lb)
- 1 tablespoon olive or vegetable oil
- ¼ cup barbecue sauce
- 2 tablespoons chili sauce
- ½ teaspoon ground cumin

1. Heat gas or charcoal grill. In shallow bowl, mix taco seasoning mix and oregano. Brush chicken with oil; sprinkle with taco seasoning mixture.

2. Place chicken on grill over medium heat. Cover grill; cook 10 to 15 minutes, turning once, until juice of chicken is clear when center of thickest part is cut (at least 165°F).

3. Meanwhile, in small microwavable bowl, mix barbecue sauce, chili sauce and cumin. Cover; microwave on High 30 to 60 seconds or until hot. Serve sauce over chicken.

1 Serving: Calories 240; Total Fat 8g (Saturated Fat 2g, Trans Fat 0g); Cholesterol 85mg; Sodium 780mg; Total Carbohydrate 11g (Dietary Fiber 0g); Protein 31g **Exchanges:** ½ Other Carbohydrate, 4½ Very Lean Meat, 1 Fat **Carbohydrate Choices:** 1

Tip To make the chicken in the oven, line a shallow baking pan with foil or spray with cooking spray. Place the coated chicken in the pan. Bake 25 to 30 minutes at 375°F, turning once, until juice of chicken is clear when center of thickest part is cut (at least 165°F).

Three-Herb Chicken

Prep Time: 1 Hour 5 Minutes • **Start to Finish:** 1 Hour 35 Minutes • Makes 4 servings

- ½ cup vegetable oil
- ½ cup lime juice
- 2 tablespoons chopped fresh or 2 teaspoons dried basil leaves
- 2 tablespoons chopped fresh or 2 teaspoons dried oregano leaves
- 2 tablespoons chopped fresh or 2 teaspoons dried thyme leaves
- 1 teaspoon onion powder
- ¼ teaspoon lemon-pepper seasoning
- 4 chicken thighs (about 1 lb)
- 4 chicken drumsticks (about 1 lb)

1 In shallow glass or plastic dish or heavy-duty resealable food-storage plastic bag, mix all ingredients except chicken. Add chicken thighs and drumsticks; turn to coat with marinade. Cover dish or seal bag; refrigerate to marinate, turning chicken occasionally, at least 30 minutes but no longer than 24 hours.

2 Heat gas or charcoal grill. Remove chicken from marinade; reserve marinade. Place chicken, skin side down, on grill over medium heat. Cover grill; cook 15 minutes. Turn chicken; brush with marinade. Cover grill; cook 15 minutes longer. Brush with marinade; cook 5 to 15 minutes longer or until juice of chicken is clear when thickest part is cut to bone (180°F). Discard any remaining marinade.

1 Serving: Calories 510; Total Fat 42g (Saturated Fat 9g, Trans Fat 0g); Cholesterol 95mg; Sodium 115mg; Total Carbohydrate 4g (Dietary Fiber 1g); Protein 30g **Exchanges:** 4½ Lean Meat, 5½ Fat **Carbohydrate Choices:** 0

Tip Microwave the chicken to partially cook it before grilling. Not only does this save time, but it can also help prevent overcooked, burned chicken. Place marinated chicken in microwavable dish with thickest parts to the outside edge. Cover with microwavable plastic wrap, folding back one corner to allow steam to escape. Microwave on High 10 to 12 minutes, rotating dish ½ turn after 5 minutes, until edges begin to cook; drain. Immediately put chicken on heated grill; grill 15 to 20 minutes.

Firecracker Chicken Drummies

Prep Time: 35 Minutes • **Start to Finish:** 1 Hour 35 Minutes • Makes 20 appetizers

2 tablespoons chili powder
1½ teaspoons dried oregano leaves
1¼ teaspoons ground red pepper (cayenne)
1 teaspoon garlic salt
1 teaspoon ground cumin
1 teaspoon pepper
2 packages (1 lb each) chicken wing drummettes
Sour cream, if desired
Paprika, if desired

1 In 1-gallon resealable food-storage plastic bag, place all ingredients except chicken, sour cream and paprika. Seal bag; shake to blend seasonings. Add chicken; seal bag and shake to coat with seasonings. Refrigerate at least 1 hour to marinate but no longer than 24 hours.

2 Heat gas or charcoal grill. Place chicken in grill basket (grill "wok"). Place basket on grill over medium heat. Cover grill; cook 20 to 25 minutes, shaking basket to turn chicken after 10 minutes, until juice of chicken is clear when thickest part is cut to bone (180°F).

3 Serve chicken with sour cream sprinkled with paprika.

1 Appetizer: Calories 50; Total Fat 2.5g (Saturated Fat 1g, Trans Fat 0g); Cholesterol 20mg; Sodium 70mg; Total Carbohydrate 0g (Dietary Fiber 0g); Protein 6g **Exchanges:** 1 Lean Meat **Carbohydrate Choices:** 0

Tip Grill baskets (grill "woks") are available at discount stores or in kitchen specialty shops.

Jerk Chicken Kabobs

Prep Time: 25 Minutes • **Start to Finish:** 1 Hour 25 Minutes • Makes 6 kabobs

- 6 boneless skinless chicken thighs (about 1¼ lb), cut into 1-inch cubes
- ⅓ cup jerk seasoning sauce
- 1 cup canned or fresh pineapple chunks
- 2 medium red bell peppers, each cut into 12 wedges
- ½ medium onion, cut into 12 wedges, separated into chunks

1 In shallow glass or plastic dish or resealable food-storage plastic bag, mix chicken and ¼ cup of the jerk sauce. Cover dish or seal bag; refrigerate 1 hour to marinate, stirring occasionally.

2 Heat gas or charcoal grill. Drain chicken; discard marinade. On each of 6 (15-inch) metal skewers, thread chicken, pineapple, bell pepper and onion, leaving space between each piece. Brush vegetables with remaining jerk sauce.

3 Place kabobs on grill over medium heat. Cover grill; cook about 15 minutes or until chicken is no longer pink in center and vegetables are tender.

1 Kabob: Calories 210; Total Fat 8g (Saturated Fat 2.5g, Trans Fat 0g); Cholesterol 60mg; Sodium 140mg; Total Carbohydrate 14g (Dietary Fiber 1g); Protein 20g **Exchanges:** 1 Other Carbohydrate, 3 Lean Meat **Carbohydrate Choices:** 1

Tip For an easy and delicious summer supper, serve grilled kabobs with hot buttered basmati rice.

Surf and Turf

Spicy Coconut-Curry Shrimp

Prep Time: 20 Minutes • **Start to Finish:** 45 Minutes • Makes 6 servings (3 kabobs and 4 teaspoons sauce each)

- 20 bamboo skewers (6 inch)
- ¾ cup canned coconut milk (not cream of coconut)
- 2 teaspoons curry powder
- 2 teaspoons cornstarch
- 1 teaspoon honey
- ¼ teaspoon salt
- 60 uncooked medium shrimp (about 2 lb), thawed if frozen, peeled, deveined
- 2 tablespoons olive or vegetable oil
- 1 teaspoon red pepper sauce

1. Soak skewers in water at least 30 minutes before using to prevent burning. Meanwhile, heat gas or charcoal grill. In small microwavable bowl, mix coconut milk, curry powder, cornstarch, honey and salt. Microwave uncovered on High about 2 minutes, stirring every 30 seconds, until mixture bubbles and thickens; set aside.

2. In large bowl, place shrimp. Drizzle with oil and pepper sauce; toss to coat. Thread 3 shrimp on each skewer, leaving space between each.

3. Place kabobs on grill over medium heat. Cover grill; cook 4 to 6 minutes, turning once, until shrimp are pink. Serve with coconut-curry mixture.

1 Serving: Calories 210; Total Fat 11g (Saturated Fat 5g, Trans Fat 0g); Cholesterol 215mg; Sodium 370mg; Total Carbohydrate 5g (Dietary Fiber 1g); Protein 24g **Exchanges:** ½ Other Carbohydrate, 3½ Lean Meat **Carbohydrate Choices:** ½

Fish Tacos

Prep Time: 20 Minutes • **Start to Finish:** 20 Minutes • Makes 8 tacos

Tacos

- 1 lb sea bass, red snapper or other medium-firm fish fillets
- 1 tablespoon olive oil
- 1 teaspoon ground cumin or chili powder
- ½ teaspoon salt
- ¼ teaspoon pepper
- 8 soft corn tortillas (6 inch), heated as directed on package
- ¼ cup sour cream
- ½ cup chunky-style salsa

Toppings, if desired

- Shredded lettuce
- Chopped avocado
- Chopped tomato
- Chopped onion
- Chopped fresh cilantro
- Fresh lime wedges

1. Heat gas or charcoal grill. Brush fish with oil; sprinkle with cumin, salt and pepper.

2. Carefully brush additional oil on grill rack. Place fish on grill over medium heat. Cover grill; cook 5 to 7 minutes, turning once, until fish flakes easily with fork.

3. Spread one side of each tortilla with sour cream; top with fish, salsa and choice of toppings. Squeeze lime juice over tacos. Serve immediately.

1 Taco: Calories 150; Total Fat 6g (Saturated Fat 2g, Trans Fat 0g); Cholesterol 30mg; Sodium 290mg; Total Carbohydrate 12g (Dietary Fiber 1g); Protein 12g **Exchanges:** ½ Starch, ½ Other Carbohydrate, 1½ Very Lean Meat, 1 Fat **Carbohydrate Choices:** 1

Tip Make it a Mexican meal by serving these tacos with cooked brown rice tossed with chopped fresh cilantro plus watermelon wedges.

Seafood Packets with Lemon-Chive Butter

Prep Time: 40 Minutes • **Start to Finish:** 40 Minutes • Makes 8 servings

Seafood Packets

32 shell clams (littlenecks or cherrystones)

32 uncooked medium shrimp in shells (about 1¼ lb), thawed if frozen

32 sea scallops (about 2½ lb)

4 ears fresh sweet corn, husks removed, cleaned and cut into fourths

32 large cherry tomatoes

Lemon-Chive Butter

⅓ cup butter or margarine, melted

2 teaspoons grated lemon peel

2 teaspoons chopped fresh or ½ teaspoon freeze-dried chives

Fresh chive stems or chopped fresh chives, if desired

1 Heat gas or charcoal grill. Cut 8 (18 x 12-inch) sheets of heavy-duty foil; spray with cooking spray.

2 Place 4 each of clams, shrimp and scallops in center of each sheet; top each with 2 pieces of corn and 4 tomatoes. In small bowl, mix all butter ingredients. Drizzle about 2 teaspoons butter over seafood and vegetables in each packet.

3 Bring up 2 sides of foil so edges meet. Seal edges, making tight ½-inch fold; fold again, allowing space for heat circulation and expansion. Fold other sides to seal.

4 Place packets on grill over medium heat. Cover grill; cook 15 to 20 minutes, rotating packets one-half turn after 10 minutes, or until clam shells have opened, shrimp are pink, and scallops are white and opaque. (Cooking time may vary depending on ingredients selected.) Discard any clams that don't open.

5 Cut large X across top of each packet; carefully fold back foil to allow steam to escape. Top with chives.

1 Serving: Calories 300; Total Fat 10g (Saturated Fat 5g, Trans Fat 0g); Cholesterol 145mg; Sodium 350mg; Total Carbohydrate 17g (Dietary Fiber 3g); Protein 33g **Exchanges:** 1 Starch, 4 Lean Meat **Carbohydrate Choices:** 1

Tip Mussels can be substituted for the clams. If your guests don't care for either clams or mussels, just double the amount of shrimp or scallops instead.

Surf and Turf Kabobs

Prep Time: 20 Minutes • **Start to Finish:** 50 Minutes • Makes 12 kabobs

- ¾ lb boneless beef sirloin steak (¾ inch thick), trimmed of fat
- 12 uncooked deveined peeled medium or large shrimp, thawed if frozen, tail shells removed
- ½ cup teriyaki marinade and sauce (from 10-oz bottle)
- ¼ teaspoon coarsely ground pepper
- 12 bamboo skewers (4 to 6 inch)

1 Cut beef into 24 (¾-inch) pieces. In medium bowl, mix beef, shrimp and teriyaki sauce. Sprinkle with pepper. Cover; refrigerate 30 minutes to marinate, stirring frequently. Meanwhile, soak skewers in water at least 30 minutes before using to prevent burning.

2 Spray grill rack with cooking spray. Heat gas or charcoal grill. On each skewer, thread 1 beef piece, 1 shrimp and another beef piece, leaving space between each; reserve marinade.

3 Place kabobs on grill. Cover grill; cook over medium heat 5 to 6 minutes, turning once and brushing with marinade once or twice, until shrimp are pink. Discard any remaining marinade.

1 Kabob: Calories 50; Total Fat 1g (Saturated Fat 0g, Trans Fat 0g); Cholesterol 25mg; Sodium 480mg; Total Carbohydrate 2g (Dietary Fiber 0g); Protein 8g **Exchanges:** 1 Lean Meat **Carbohydrate Choices:** 0

Tip To make the kabobs in the oven, set oven control to broil. Spray broiler pan rack with cooking spray. Place kabobs on rack in broiler pan. Broil kabobs with tops 4 to 6 inches from heat 5 to 6 minutes, turning once and basting with marinade once or twice, until shrimp are pink.

Lemon-Pepper Steaks

Prep Time: 10 Minutes • **Start to Finish:** 25 Minutes • Makes 4 servings

4 beef sirloin or rib eye steaks, 1 inch thick (about 2 lb)

½ teaspoon garlic salt

¼ cup butter or margarine, melted

2 tablespoons chopped fresh or 1 tablespoon dried basil leaves

2 teaspoons lemon-pepper seasoning

2 medium bell peppers (any color), cut lengthwise in half, seeded

1 Brush grill rack with vegetable oil. Heat gas or charcoal grill.

2 Trim fat on beef steaks to ½-inch thickness if necessary. Sprinkle garlic salt over beef. In small bowl, mix butter, basil and lemon-pepper seasoning; brush over beef and bell pepper halves.

3 Place beef and bell peppers on grill. Cover grill; cook over medium heat 12 to 16 minutes for medium beef doneness, turning once. Brush tops of steaks with butter mixture. Cut bell peppers into strips; serve over beef.

1 Serving: Calories 530; Total Fat 36g (Saturated Fat 15g, Trans Fat 2g); Cholesterol 165mg; Sodium 470mg; Total Carbohydrate 5g (Dietary Fiber 1g); Protein 45g **Exchanges:** 1 Vegetable, 6 Medium-Fat Meat, 1 Fat **Carbohydrate Choices:** ½

Tip One of the best ways to keep steaks moist and juicy is to make sure the grill is hot before adding the steaks. A hot grill quickly sears the outside of the meat and seals in the juices.

Pork Ribs with Smoky Barbecue Sauce

Prep Time: 30 Minutes • **Start to Finish:** 1 Hour 40 Minutes • Makes 4 servings

Ribs

- 2 racks (2 lb each) pork back ribs (not cut into serving pieces)
- 1 tablespoon vegetable oil
- 4 teaspoons chopped fresh or 1½ teaspoons dried thyme leaves

Sauce

- ½ cup ketchup
- ¼ cup water
- 3 tablespoons packed brown sugar
- 2 tablespoons white vinegar
- 2 teaspoons celery seed
- ¼ teaspoon liquid smoke
- ¼ teaspoon red pepper sauce

1 Brush meaty side of ribs with oil; sprinkle with thyme. Heat gas or charcoal grill for indirect cooking. For two-burner gas grill, heat one burner to medium; place pork, meaty side up, on unheated side. For one-burner gas grill, place pork, meaty side up, on grill over low heat. For charcoal grill, move medium coals to edge of firebox; place pork, meaty side up, on grill rack over drip pan.

2 Cover grill; cook 1 hour to 1 hour 10 minutes or until tender and no longer pink next to bones. Meanwhile, in 1-quart saucepan, mix all sauce ingredients; heat to boiling. Reduce heat; simmer uncovered 15 minutes, stirring occasionally. Brush sauce over pork 2 or 3 times during last 15 minutes of grilling. Heat any remaining sauce to boiling; boil and stir 1 minute. Cut pork into 4 serving pieces. Serve with sauce.

1 Serving: Calories 960; Total Fat 70g (Saturated Fat 25g, Trans Fat 0g); Cholesterol 265mg; Sodium 550mg; Total Carbohydrate 18g (Dietary Fiber 0g); Protein 64g **Exchanges:** 1 Other Carbohydrate, 9 Medium-Fat Meat, 5 Fat **Carbohydrate Choices:** 1

Sizzling Sides

Easy Vegetables

Prep Time: 25 Minutes • **Start to Finish:** 1 Hour 25 Minutes • Makes 6 servings

12 pattypan squash (about 1 inch in diameter) or 2 medium zucchini, each cut into 1-inch pieces

2 medium red or green bell peppers, each cut into 6 pieces

1 large red onion, cut into ½-inch slices

⅓ cup Italian dressing

Freshly ground pepper, if desired

1 In 13 x 9-inch (3-quart) glass baking dish, place squash, bell peppers and onion. Pour dressing over vegetables. Cover; let stand 1 hour to blend flavors.

2 Heat gas or charcoal grill. Remove vegetables from marinade; reserve marinade. Place squash and bell peppers in grill basket (grill "wok"). Place grill basket on grill over medium heat. Cover grill; cook 5 minutes.

3 Add onion to grill basket. Cover grill; cook 5 to 10 minutes longer, turning and brushing vegetables with marinade 2 or 3 times, until tender. Sprinkle with pepper.

1 Serving: Calories 110; Total Fat 6g (Saturated Fat 0.5g, Trans Fat 0g); Cholesterol 0mg; Sodium 120mg; Total Carbohydrate 11g (Dietary Fiber 3g); Protein 2g **Exchanges:** ½ Other Carbohydrate, 1 Vegetable, 1 Fat **Carbohydrate Choices:** 1

Greek Summer Squash

Prep Time: 20 Minutes • **Start to Finish:** 20 Minutes • Makes 8 servings

- 2 medium zucchini, unpeeled, cut into 2 x ½-inch strips
- 2 medium yellow summer squash, unpeeled, cut into 2 x ½-inch strips
- ¼ cup purchased Greek vinaigrette salad dressing
- ¼ to ½ teaspoon crushed red pepper flakes
- 2 medium tomatoes, chopped
- 2 tablespoons crumbled feta cheese

1. Heat gas or charcoal grill. In large bowl, combine zucchini, summer squash, salad dressing and pepper flakes; toss to coat. Place zucchini and squash in grill basket (grill "wok"). Reserve dressing mixture in bowl.

2. Place grill basket on gas grill over medium heat or on charcoal grill 4 to 6 inches from medium coals. Cook 10 to 12 minutes, stirring occasionally, or until vegetables are tender.

3. Add tomatoes to dressing mixture; toss to coat. Add warm zucchini and squash; toss to coat. Sprinkle with cheese.

1 Serving: Calories 70; Total Fat 4g (Saturated Fat 1g, Trans Fat 0g); Cholesterol 5mg; Sodium 100mg; Total Carbohydrate 6g (Dietary Fiber 1g); Protein 2g **Exchanges:** ½ Starch, 1 Fat **Carbohydrate Choices:** ½

Parmesan, Asparagus and Mushrooms

Prep Time: 25 Minutes • **Start to Finish:** 25 Minutes • Makes 4 servings

1 lb fresh asparagus spears

1 package (6 oz) sliced fresh portabella mushrooms

¼ cup balsamic vinaigrette dressing

2 tablespoons chopped fresh basil leaves

¼ cup shredded fresh Parmesan cheese

1 Heat gas or charcoal grill. In large shallow dish, toss asparagus, mushrooms and dressing. Place vegetables in grill basket (grill "wok").

2 Place basket on grill over medium heat. Cover grill; cook vegetables over medium heat 8 to 12 minutes, shaking basket or stirring vegetables occasionally, until asparagus is crisp-tender. Sprinkle vegetables with basil and cheese. Cover grill; cook 3 to 4 minutes longer or until cheese is slightly melted.

1 Serving: Calories 120; Total Fat 9g (Saturated Fat 2g, Trans Fat 0g); Cholesterol 0mg; Sodium 270mg; Total Carbohydrate 5g (Dietary Fiber 1g); Protein 5g **Exchanges:** 1 Vegetable, ½ High-Fat Meat, 1 Fat **Carbohydrate Choices:** 0

Tip When grilling asparagus, the size of the spears and variation in grill fires affect how quickly this vegetable cooks. Cook the spears just until crisp-tender.

Sizzling Sides • **23**

Corn with Herb Butter

Prep Time: 30 Minutes • **Start to Finish:** 30 Minutes • Makes 6 servings

¼ cup butter

2 tablespoons chopped fresh chives

½ teaspoon garlic salt

6 ears fresh sweet corn, husks removed, cleaned

¼ cup grated Parmesan cheese

1 Heat gas or charcoal grill. Cut 30 x 18-inch sheet of heavy-duty foil. In small microwavable bowl, place butter, chives and garlic salt. Microwave uncovered on High 15 to 20 seconds or until butter is melted.

2 Brush butter mixture over each ear of corn. Place corn on center of foil. Pour any remaining butter mixture over corn. Sprinkle with cheese. Bring 2 sides of foil up over corn so edges meet. Seal edges, making tight ½-inch fold; fold again, allowing space for heat circulation and expansion. Fold other sides to seal.

3 Place packet on grill over low heat. Cover grill; cook 12 to 18 minutes, rotating packet ½ turn after every 6 minutes, until corn is tender. To serve, cut large X across top of packet; carefully fold back foil to allow steam to escape.

1 Serving: Calories 210; Total Fat 10g (Saturated Fat 6g, Trans Fat 0g); Cholesterol 25mg; Sodium 220mg; Total Carbohydrate 25g (Dietary Fiber 4g); Protein 5g **Exchanges:** 1½ Starch, 2 Fat **Carbohydrate Choices:** 1½

Herbed New Potatoes

Prep Time: 25 Minutes • **Start to Finish:** 25 Minutes • Makes 4 servings

Sauce
- ⅓ cup sour cream
- 1 tablespoon chopped fresh or ½ teaspoon dried rosemary leaves, crumbled
- ¼ teaspoon lemon-pepper seasoning
- ⅛ teaspoon garlic powder

Potatoes
- 2 tablespoons olive or vegetable oil
- 1 tablespoon chopped fresh or ½ teaspoon dried parsley flakes
- 1 tablespoon chopped fresh or ½ teaspoon dried rosemary leaves, crumbled
- ½ teaspoon lemon-pepper seasoning
- ¼ teaspoon salt
- 8 small red potatoes, cut into quarters

1 Heat gas or charcoal grill. In small bowl, mix all sauce ingredients. Cover; refrigerate until serving.

2 In large bowl, mix remaining ingredients except potatoes. Add potatoes; toss to coat. Place potatoes in grill basket (grill "wok").

3 Place basket on grill over medium heat. Cover grill; cook 10 to 15 minutes, shaking basket or stirring potatoes occasionally, until tender. Serve potatoes with sauce.

1 Serving: Calories 270; Total Fat 11g (Saturated Fat 3.5g, Trans Fat 0g); Cholesterol 15mg; Sodium 240mg; Total Carbohydrate 40g (Dietary Fiber 4g); Protein 5g **Exchanges:** 2 Starch, ½ Other Carbohydrate, 2 Fat **Carbohydrate Choices:** 2½

Metric Conversion Guide

Volume

U.S. Units	Canadian Metric	Australian Metric
¼ teaspoon	1 mL	1 ml
½ teaspoon	2 mL	2 ml
1 teaspoon	5 mL	5 ml
1 tablespoon	15 mL	20 ml
¼ cup	50 mL	60 ml
⅓ cup	75 mL	80 ml
½ cup	125 mL	125 ml
⅔ cup	150 mL	170 ml
¾ cup	175 mL	190 ml
1 cup	250 mL	250 ml
1 quart	1 liter	1 liter
1½ quarts	1.5 liters	1.5 liters
2 quarts	2 liters	2 liters
2½ quarts	2.5 liters	2.5 liters
3 quarts	3 liters	3 liters
4 quarts	4 liters	4 liters

Weight

U.S. Units	Canadian Metric	Australian Metric
1 ounce	30 grams	30 grams
2 ounces	55 grams	60 grams
3 ounces	85 grams	90 grams
4 ounces (¼ pound)	115 grams	125 grams
8 ounces (½ pound)	225 grams	225 grams
16 ounces (1 pound)	455 grams	500 grams
1 pound	455 grams	0.5 kilogram

Note: The recipes in this cookbook have not been developed or tested using metric measures. When converting recipes to metric, some variations in quality may be noted.

Measurements

Inches	Centimeters
1	2.5
2	5.0
3	7.5
4	10.0
5	12.5
6	15.0
7	17.5
8	20.5
9	23.0
10	25.5
11	28.0
12	30.5
13	33.0

Temperatures

Fahrenheit	Celsius
32°	0°
212°	100°
250°	120°
275°	140°
300°	150°
325°	160°
350°	180°
375°	190°
400°	200°
425°	220°
450°	230°
475°	240°
500°	260°

Recipe Testing and Calculating Nutrition Information

Recipe Testing:

- Large eggs and 2% milk were used unless otherwise indicated.
- Fat-free, low-fat, low-sodium or lite products were not used unless indicated.
- No nonstick cookware and bakeware were used unless otherwise indicated. No dark-colored, black or insulated bakeware was used.
- When a pan is specified, a metal pan was used; a baking dish or pie plate means ovenproof glass was used.
- An electric hand mixer was used for mixing only when mixer speeds are specified.

Calculating Nutrition:

- The first ingredient was used wherever a choice is given, such as ⅓ cup sour cream or plain yogurt.
- The first amount was used wherever a range is given, such as 3- to 3½-pound whole chicken.
- The first serving number was used wherever a range is given, such as 4 to 6 servings.
- "If desired" ingredients were not included.
- Only the amount of a marinade or frying oil that is absorbed was included.

America's most trusted cookbook is better than ever!

- 1,100 all-new photos, including hundreds of step-by-step images
- More than 1,500 recipes, with hundreds of inspiring variations and creative "mini" recipes for easy cooking ideas
- Brand-new features
- Gorgeous new design

Get the best edition of the *Betty Crocker Cookbook* today!

www.ingramcontent.com/pod-product-compliance
Lightning Source LLC
Chambersburg PA
CBHW071418290426
44108CB00014B/1881